Known Facts of Time Travel

Mohammed Azzam

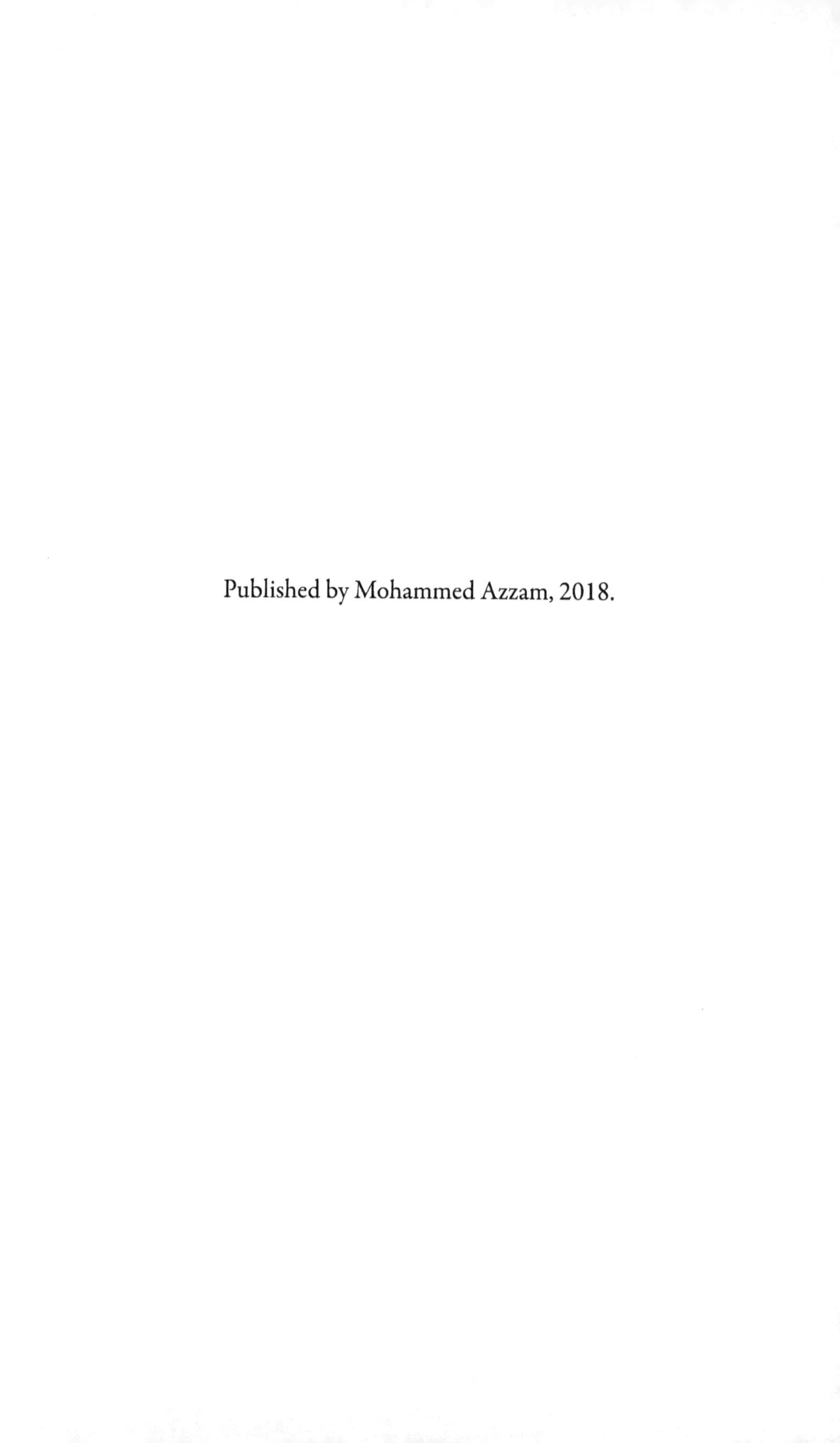

Published by Mohammed Azzam, 2018.

While every precaution has been taken in the preparation of this book, the publisher assumes no responsibility for errors or omissions, or for damages resulting from the use of the information contained herein.

KNOWN FACTS OF TIME TRAVEL

First edition. November 20, 2018.

Copyright © 2018 Mohammed Azzam.

Written by Mohammed Azzam.

Also by Mohammed Azzam

Inflation and Variable Interest
Virtual Reality and Augmented Reality Safety Rules
Known Facts of Time Travel

Watch for more at https://books2read.com/ap/
R3Lm35/Mohammed-Azzam.

Preface

Do you know, time traveler, the impact of time traveling over your personal life? This book discusses this question and of course, it will continue building our hypothetical time travel machine based upon General Relativity Theory and Special Relativity Theory. Because I wanted my last book "Virtual Reality and Augmented Reality Safety Rules" to be as simple as possible, I couldn't continue building such a time travel machine. As you know the Relativity Theory is quite complex! I had to write another book to take off some of "Virtual Reality and Augmented Reality Safety Rules" book's complexity.

This book begins with explaining some known methods for time travel. It also explains "Humanity Timeline Theory" in more details. It also describes the relationship between "Humanity Timeline Theory" and Relativity Theory.

Then it starts our journey to build a time travel machine by discussing the available technology nowadays that suits time travel. Then it moves to discuss the characteristics of time travel, so we can understand time travel better. Why you failed to solve a problem? Because you need a better understanding for that problem, so you can solve it!

After that it discusses a hypothetical time travel machine model based upon both some known methods of time travel and Relativity Theory!

Finally, if you feel your head is spinning right now, you may not continue reading this book.

How to Time Travel?

Here you are some known methods for traveling through time:

First, Speed:

According to Einstein's theory of special relativity, when you travel at speeds approaching the speed of light, time slows down for you relative to the outside world.

This is not a just a conjecture or thought experiment, it's been measured using twin atomic clocks. Physicists have put one in a jet aircraft, while the other is stationary on Earth. Physicists have shown that a flying clock ticks slower, because of its speed. In the case of the aircraft, the effect is minuscule. But If you were in a spaceship travelling at 90% of the speed of light, you'd experience time passing about 2.6 times slower than it was back on Earth. And the closer you get to the speed of light, the more extreme the time-travel.

The highest speeds achieved through any human technology are probably the protons whizzing around the Large Hadron Collider at 99.9999991% of the speed of light. Using special relativity, we can calculate one second for the proton is equivalent to 27,777,778 seconds, or about 11 months, for us.

Amazingly, particle physicists must take this time dilation into account when they are dealing with particles that decay. In the lab, muon particles typically decay in 2.2 microseconds. But fast-moving muons, such as those created when cosmic rays strike the upper atmosphere, take 10 times longer to disintegrate.

Second, Gravity:

The next method is also inspired by Einstein. According to his theory of general relativity, the stronger the gravity you feel, the slower time moves. As you get closer to the center of the Earth, for example, the strength of gravity increases. Time runs slower for your feet than your head.

Again, this effect has been measured. In 2010, physicists at the US National Institute of Standards and Technology (NIST) placed two atomic clocks on shelves, one 33 centimeters above the other, and measured the difference in their rate of ticking. The lower one ticked slower because it feels a slightly stronger gravity.

To travel to the far future, all we need is a region of extremely strong gravity, such as a black hole. The closer you get to the event horizon, the slower time moves, but it's risky business. If you cross the boundary, you can never escape. And anyway, the effect is not that strong so it's probably not worth the trip. Assuming you had the technology to travel the vast distances to reach a black hole which is about 3,000 light years away for the nearest one, the time dilation through travelling would be far greater than any time dilation through orbiting the black hole itself.

Third, Wormholes:

General relativity also allows for the possibility for shortcuts through spacetime, known as wormholes, which might be able to bridge distances of a billion light years or more, or different points in time. Many physicists, including Stephen Hawking, believe wormholes are constantly popping in and out of existence at the quantum scale, which is far smaller than atoms. The trick would be to capture one and inflate it to human scales, a feat that would require a huge amount of energy, but which might just be possible, in theory.

Attempts to prove this either way have failed, ultimately because of the incompatibility between general relativity and quantum mechanics.

Fourth, Suspended animation:

Another way to travel to the future may be to slow your perception of time by slowing down, or stopping, your bodily processes and then restarting them later.

Bacterial spores can live for millions of years in a state of suspended animation, until the right conditions of temperature, moisture and food kick start their metabolisms again. Some mammals, such as bears and squirrels, can slow down their metabolism during hibernation, dramatically reducing their cells' requirement for food and oxygen. Could humans ever do the same?

Though completely stopping your metabolism is probably far beyond our current technology, some scientists are working towards achieving inducing a short-term hibernation state lasting at least a few hours. This might be just enough time to get a person through a medical emergency, such as a cardiac arrest, before they can reach the hospital.

In 2005, American scientists demonstrated a way to slow the metabolism of mice which do not hibernate by exposing them to minute doses of hydrogen sulfide, which binds to the same cell receptors as oxygen. The core body temperature of the mice dropped to 13 °C and metabolism decreased 10-fold. After six hours the mice could be reanimated without ill effects. Unfortunately, similar experiments on sheep and pigs were not successful, suggesting the method might not work for larger animals.

Another method, which induces a hypothermic hibernation by replacing the blood with a cold saline solution, has worked on pigs and is currently undergoing human clinical trials in Pittsburgh.

Modern technology is using the speed method already, as it will be explained later. We could combine speed method and gravity method together to build a time travel machine. So, there is no need to wait for a wormhole to catch. Yes, I think scientists have thrown a fishline and they are just waiting for a wormhole to catch, so they can start building a time travel machine. The final method mentioned previously which is suspended animation is more likely to be an anti-aging technique rather than a time travel method!

Humanity Timeline Theory

Let's consider an LCD, yes that LCD you use at home to watch your favorite programs and serials! Let's look at what it consists of? It's made of a screen which is glass, glass is made of sand. Also, it is made of some chips which are made of silicon, silicon is sand. Your LCD includes some printed circuits that's made of copper and plastic, plastic is a polymer that's made of oil. This concludes that the main raw material that your LCD is made of are: sand, copper, oil and may be some gold!

Don't you think that this raw material isn't there on earth since the stone age? Yes, those raw material used to make your own LCD particularly were on Earth since the stone age, so why that stone age man couldn't make himself an LCD, although LCD's raw material did exist at his time? The answer is a stone age man did not of course know how to make it, so he did not make himself an LCD. He did not even know how to turn sand into glass!

Why, unfortunately, do all nowadays airplanes have windows on their cockpits? The answer is airplane manufacturers do not know how to use augmented reality right. I bit they do not even know what it is!

So, the point is it's the "know how" that makes the difference between our modern age and the stone age! Yes, even a genius stone age man would be treated as a person with intellectual disability, if he came to our modern age! Thus, the differences between human history timeline ages is all about the "know how" the more knowledge humanity has gathered the closer they are to our modern age, and vice versa! Now, humanity timeline theory is as follows:

Human history timeline ages are a scale of how much the humanity has accumulated of our modern age knowledge, the more knowledge humanity has gathered of our modern age knowledge the closer they are to our modern age, and vice versa!

The paragraph above is a social theory called "Humanity Timeline Theory" and that paragraph is about the broad human history timeline as a whole while the discussion about the single human timeline is called "Virtual Reality and Augmented Reality Timeline Theory"! For more information please read the book "Virtual Reality and Augmented Reality Safety Rules".

Now let's consider if someone managed to build a time travel machine in the year 2100AD and he traveled back one thousand years ago, would be his watch's date still 2100AD or not? The answer is yes, amazingly his watch would be still pointing to 2100AD although it would be 1100AD. How?

Because watches or clocks are just counters that count forward that's to say 1,2,3, ...etc. and it happens by coincidence that this count matches the right time, yes surprisingly there are no strings attached between your watch and human history timeline of course! That time traveler really would need to set his watch again to 1100AD because his watch is just a forward counter that counts seconds forward only! It's the same thing even if he used an atomic clock.

Alas, there is no known device to determine where you are on the human history timeline! Even an atomic clock is not suitable for time travel! This leads to the only known way to determine where you are on the human history timeline is the human mind judgment on the sequence of events he had previously. That's to say: your position on the human history timeline is only judged by your mind! How?

Let's consider that back-time traveler, his watch is useless of course, so he will try to calculate how much people around him have accumulated of his age's knowledge, that's to say he will compare that age's humanity knowledge to his age's humanity knowledge which is our modern age. the more knowledge those people around him have gathered of our modern age's knowledge the closer they are to our modern age, and vice versa! As stated by "Humanity Timeline Theory".

Simply, "Humanity Timeline Theory" explains how our minds do judge our position through human history timeline.

In simple words, if that back-time traveler saw people around him riding cars to go to work, he would think that his time travel machine has failed, but if he saw them riding horses to go to work, he would think his time travel machine has succeeded!

Now let's consider if someone managed to build a time travel machine in the year 2100AD and traveled forward one thousand years, would be his watch's date still 2100AD or not? The answer is yes, amazingly his watch would be still pointing to 2100AD although it would be 3100AD. How?

Because his watch is just a forward counter that counts seconds forward only! It's the same thing even if he used an atomic clock. It does not leap seconds or years, that time traveler really would need to set his watch again to 3100AD because there are no strings attached between his watch and human history timeline of course!

Now that forward time traveler would need to calculate how much people around him have accumulated of his age's knowledge, that's to say he will compare that age's humanity knowledge to his age's humanity knowledge which is our modern age. The more knowledge those people around him have gathered of our modern age's knowledge the closer they are to our modern age!

In simple words, if that forward time traveler saw people around him riding cars to go to work, he would think that his time travel machine has failed but if he saw them riding UFOs to go to work, he would think his time travel machine has succeeded!

But if that forward time traveler saw people around him riding horses to go to work, he would think that his time travel machine has failed. Although, it really would be 3100AD and people around him are riding horses to go to work because a nuclear war that took place sometime before 3100AD, this nuclear war has taken every known technology to the ground! As you can see using mind judgment to exactly determine your human history timeline position is tricky!

I hope this theory will be the first step for inventing a time travel machine because a better understanding of the problem always helps to find a solution to that problem. I have not seen serious steps taken to build a time travel machine although the modern technology is so close to building one!

The Relationship Between "Humanity Timeline Theory" and Relativity Theory

Previous chapter concludes there is no known device to determine where you are on the human history timeline. a clock is not time, it just happens that a clock indicates the current time by coincidence, clocks are a relative measure of time, they are not an absolute measure of time. Clocks measure time relative to a previously adjusted value of time, while age of planet earth is an absolute measure of time for planet earth. In the case of the time travel problem, the time that we do care about is the age of planet earth because it's an absolute measure of time.

What's the age of planet earth? Age of planet earth is how many times planet earth circled around the sun. Thus, the age of planet earth projects time as a distant displacement as Einstein would like. Because in Special Relativity Theory, time and space are not independent!

So "Humanity Timeline Theory" states that the real time is the age of planet earth in accordance with Special Relativity Theory. I would like to call "Age of Planet Earth" is the relationship between "Humanity Timeline Theory" and "Special Relativity Theory". I would not like to call it an assumption.

It also states "mind judgment" is the only known way to determine where you are on the human history timeline, but mind judgment can be tricky, a time traveler cannot depend on neither mind judgment nor his watch to determine where he is on the human history timeline exactly.

As stated by "Humanity Timeline Theory", The first step to build a time travel machine is that we need some genius to invent a device that can tell exactly what year it is, we are living in, after examining some tree or some rocks or some soil. Because, a time traveler cannot depend on his watch or even his sense "mind judgment" to tell where he is on the human history timeline exactly.

This machine must read the real time which is earth's age by depending on something that cannot be tricked like some soil for instance. That's to say the age of soil is equivalent to time traveler's current position on human history timeline. Yes, this should be the idea behind such machine to determine the exact position of a time traveler on human history timeline. But how?

This problem resembles "How are fossils dated?", Scientists combine several well-tested techniques to find out the ages of fossils. The most important are relative dating and radiometric dating.

What is relative dating? It is a process in which fossils and layers of rock are placed in order from oldest to youngest. What is radiometric dating? It is a process in which the actual ages of certain types of rocks are calculated. we are interested in radiometric dating because we need an exact position of a time traveler.

After scientists learned that the nuclear decay of radioactive elements takes place at a predictable rate, they realized that the traces of radioactive elements present in certain types of rocks, such as hardened lava and tuff which is from compacted volcanic ash, those types of rocks could be analyzed chemically to determine the ages of those rocks. This chemical analysis is called radiometric dating, radiometric dating can determine the age of a rock in years. So, this machine might use radiometric dating to at least tell precisely what year it is after examining the soil or something.

This machine is not only needed to determine the exact position of a time traveler on human history timeline, but it might be used to determine the exact real time on Mars as humanity will spread over more one planet. Of course, there is a time difference between Earth and Mars because the real current time on Mars is currently the age of planet Mars.

So, a time traveler should always use a radiometric dating equipment to determine his or her exact position on human history timeline.

Nowadays Time Travel

If you think that, we are all time travelers as we are swept along in the current of time, from past to future, at a rate of one hour per hour. Then you are wrong! Yes, we are all time travelers as we are swept along in the current of time, from past to future, but everybody is swept along in the current of time by deferent rates!

Let us consider that, you are in a race with your neighbor, the race is all about who is going to get to the town center first, you are racing on foot, while she is racing in her car. Of course, she will win the race even if she took multiple deferent paths to the town center. Why? Because she is swept along in the current of time, from past to future, at a higher rate than yours! Path or distance does not mater in the previous example, your neighbor's rate of sweeping along in the current of time is the reason why she is the winner!

Let us consider, if you traveled from san Francisco to New York. If your airplane departure time is 10:00am, you would arrive at New York 6:00pm for sure, although you have spent five hours in an airplane only. Why? The answer is because there is a timing deference between the two cities. Now, why you didn't put that timing deference to use before your departure from San Francisco? Because you didn't travel yet. Now, why you should put that timing deference to use after your arrival at New York? Because you did travel both a distance and a time interval simultaneously!

Take care, you have spent five hours in an airplane only, then when you get out of the airplane you find out it has been eight hours since you get in the airplane, yes do the math, don't be afraid, math is fun. Congratulations, you have traveled three hours in time! You used the speed method as mentioned in the first chapter when you have traveled those three hours in time. Keep in your mind, you never travel a distance only, you must travel in time also. Because in Special Relativity Theory, time and space are not independent!

This book never denies timing differences between cities, it just discusses a precise description for your traveling action. The purpose of this book is: Never think of traveling in time independently, it is always the case that your travel in time is accompanied by a distance traveled and vice versa! As stated by Special Relativity Theory.

Jules Verne's time machine is called airplane nowadays. Can't you see, modern technology is so close to build a time travel machine! Your airline might comment on those three hours traveled in time as follows: "we are terribly sorry, we didn't mean it really, it was the last thing on our minds. Please, forgive us!"

Of course, the first thing you need to do after you get out of the airplane is to set your watch to the correct time which is New York's time. Humanity Timeline Theory states that your social behavior will not change no matter how much you have traveled in time. For example, your social behavior if you have traveled in time for few hours is the same as your social behavior if you have traveled in time for one thousand years, the first thing you would need to do after you have traveled in time for one thousand years is to set your watch to the correct date. It's just that simple!

Nowadays technology allows few hours of time travel. Which is not satisfying for the most of you. Why is nobody noticed that timing interval traveled in time? Firstly, this timing interval traveled isn't satisfying. Secondly, you are focused on the distance traveled, you didn't mean to time travel. Besides, the most of you think of time-travel as you will travel in time only with no displacement in space, that is quite wrong. This contradicts Special Relativity Theory.

In the case of the airplanes, the effect of speed on time travel is minuscule. But this minuscule effect causes few hours of time travel, as explained before. So, we just need to boost that minuscule effect to travel in time by more than few hours! We need to push these limits a little bit, this will be discussed later in this book.

This chapter concludes that a realistic scenario of time travel is: For example, you might travel by airplane from San Francisco at 2100AD then you will arrive in New York at 3100AD. Or you might travel by airplane from San Francisco at 2100AD then you will arrive in New York in 18th century. You cannot travel in time while you are in your place, you must be traveling a distance and a timing interval simultaneously. If you imagine that you can travel in time by pressing a bottom, you are quite wrong. If you don't displace, you will not move in time as stated by Special Relativity Theory.

Characteristics of Time Travel

Let us discuss the general characteristics of time travel:

First, no matter duplication:

Time travel doesn't involve matter duplication, that's to say there won't be another copy of you someplace else after you have traveled in time from our present day.

Let us consider that you had an important term exam at your high school ten years ago. You have managed some how to travel back in time to the time that exam was taken, but you traveled back at the time you were taking that term exam to Disney Land instead of your high school wrongfully! What do you think will happen?

If you thought that there will be another copy of you taking that term exam while you are in Disney Land, then you thought wrong! There would be only one copy of you in Disney Land only! What about the other you that were in your high school? The answer is, you simply managed to shift that other copy of you from your high school to Disney Land while you were traveling in time, this is correct for two reasons: First, time travel doesn't involve matter duplication. Second, it is always the case that your travel in time is accompanied by a distance traveled and vice versa! As stated by Special Relativity Theory.

Second, time travel alter history:

Let us consider the previously mentioned high school example where you accidently traveled to Disney Land instead of your high school. It was explained that you have shifted yourself from your high school to Disney Land, right then your term exam's result will be "no show"!

Yes, time travel does change history. You would better laser target your past place in history to minimize your loss, it is not as being believed that you cannot meet yourself in your past because you and your copy would be vanished. No, there is only one copy of you really, the other copy would shift to your new place in history!

Third, time travel alter future also:

As mentioned before, time travel does change history. This inspires us that time travel does change future too, this is correct for two reasons: First, time travel doesn't involve matter duplication. Second, it is always the case that your travel in time is accompanied by a distance traveled and vice versa! As stated by Special Relativity Theory.

Fourth, your present-day community opinion:

If you succeeded to time travel from present day, it would look like as you have disappeared in the present day. You would keep it like that if you were still somewhere in time. Because, time travel doesn't involve matter duplication, you would not pop out again, unless you traveled back to the present day.

So, your community opinion about your time travel trip is: it would look like as you have disappeared for a while then you popped out again. Yes, that is correct, let us consider: you are watching an airplane flying in the sky, it will keep going bigger and bigger as it is coming closer to your local time. Then, it will keep going smaller and smaller until it is vanished, because it passed away from your local time. This explains why it would look like as you have disappeared in the present day.

Fifth, your somewhere in time community opinion:

If you traveled backward in time, you would be treated as a super genius person while if you traveled forward in time, you would be treated as a person with profound intellectual disability.

Yes, that is correct as stated by Humanity Timeline Theory: " Human history timeline ages are a scale of how much the humanity has accumulated of our modern age knowledge, the more knowledge humanity has gathered of our modern age knowledge the closer they are to our modern age, and vice versa!".

For example, let us consider nowadays educated thirteen years-old kid and a thirteen years-old kid in the 10th century, nowadays kid knows what's a square root is, while that 10th century's kid can hardly count his numbers. If both kids swapped position in time, 10th century's community would tell about nowadays kid that "she is genius, could you imagine that she knows that magic spell which is called "the square root"!". While if a person of nowadays community asked that 10th century's kid "What is the square root of four?", naturally, she would answer "w... w... what?" because she lacks more than one thousand years of humanity knowledge! Of course, everybody nowadays would think this 10th century's kid is a so idiot girl.

Sixth, never think of traveling in time independently:

The purpose of this book is: Never think of traveling in time independently, it is always the case that your travel in time is accompanied by a distance traveled and vice versa! As stated by Special Relativity Theory.

Besides, the deeper you want to travel in time, the more distance you would need to displace and vice versa. It is obviously that you cannot travel in time while you are in your place, you must be traveling a distance and a timing interval simultaneously, so you cannot travel from San Francisco 2100AD to San Francisco 3100AD, for example.

Seventh, time travel is a side effect:

Really, time travel is a side effect of nowadays airplanes' fast travel. Why? because it cannot be controlled, besides, they don't mean it really. It is also a side effect of nowadays ships' fast travel. Discussing travel by airplanes doesn't mean we should neglect ships, ships are also involved.

Hypothetical Time Travel Machine Model

According to Einstein's theory of General Relativity, the stronger the gravity you feel, the slower time moves. As you get closer to the center of the Earth, for example, the strength of gravity increases. Time runs slower for your feet than your head.

General Relativity Theory inspires Humanity Timeline Theory that the gravity's change you feel, accelerates your movement in time. In other words, Humanity Timeline Theory assumes, you need a change in gravity's strength to accelerate your movement in time, no change in gravity's strength means no movement in time.

One possibly good movie's manuscript is about a protagonist who takes an airplane to travel to her home town, after her airplane takes off, it meets a region of extremely strong gravity while it's in the way to its destination. Because there is a large meteor passing very near to planet earth. This region of extremely strong gravity forces her airplane to travel in time accidently, right then her airplane travels to her home town one hundred years after apocalypse. Because there is no civilization at one hundred years after apocalypse, her airplane is forced to land. After this horrible forced landing, she struggles to get back to her home time! Of course, she needs to reverse what happened to her airplane, so she can return to her home time. She might wait for another meteor to pass very near to planet earth, or she might look for a region of extremely strong gravity. Naturally, she cannot do that alone, she needs to team up with a scientist who explains to her how the hell she has traveled in time. She and this scientist who helps her have fallen in love of course, this situation leads to the following questions: Are they going to travel together back to her home time? Is she going to abandon him to travel back to her home time alone? The answer to these questions is left for the director of course!

This scenario is possible according to the theory of General Relativity. This scenario also combines both speed and gravity methods of time travel discussed in the first chapter. Her airplane is accelerated to move in time by both airplane's fast speed and a region of extremely strong gravity. Humanity Timeline Theory assumes this region of extremely strong gravity to be equivalent to a change in gravity's strength.

This scenario also can be the scientific explanation of the vanishing of Amelia Earhart over the ocean. Because that's what it would look like. If you have leaped some years in time, it would look like as you have vanished in the present day. Of course, your airline won't mention that you could accidently arrive your destination one hundred years before your departure time as stated by the special relativity theory. Because you don't travel a distance only, you do travel in time too.

Nowadays jet engines do throttle a massive amount of gases to change the pressure of an airplane's surrounding air. This change of airplane's surrounding air pressure is what makes airplanes fly.

This concludes that, we need a machine that changes the pressure of its surrounding air for space travel in addition to changing the gravity's strength of its surrounding air for time travel. This machine might be capable of leaping some years in time!

One possible travel machine's model, that might travel in time for more than few hours, is of course an airplane that has a jet engine that simultaneously changes the pressure of its surrounding air for space travel, in addition to changing the gravity's strength of its surrounding air for time travel. According to the Relativity Theory such engine will require a lot of energy to operate. This jet engine might be using a nuclear reactor to operate instead of regular airplane's fuel. That is why nowadays airplanes are not likely to travel in time for more than few hours.

A time travel machine will most likely travel in air rather than sea, because traveling in air requires less energy than in sea since density of air is much less than water. That is why nowadays nuclear submarines are not likely to travel in time for more than few hours. Of course, this time travel machine should use a radiometric dating equipment to determine its exact position on human history timeline.

Finally, I wish someone finds this theory useful and I wish you all a happy time travel trip!

Don't miss out!

Visit the website below and you can sign up to receive emails whenever Mohammed Azzam publishes a new book. There's no charge and no obligation.

https://books2read.com/r/B-A-QOZG-KWFW

BOOKS 2 READ

Connecting independent readers to independent writers.

Also by Mohammed Azzam

Inflation and Variable Interest
Virtual Reality and Augmented Reality Safety Rules
Known Facts of Time Travel

Watch for more at https://books2read.com/ap/
R3Lm35/Mohammed-Azzam.

About the Author

Hello, my name is Mohammed Azzam :
    E–Mail : smartspecies@hotmail.com
    Occupation : software-engineer.
    Education : Faculty of Engineering - I have a B.A. in
Automatic Control Engineering.
    Certification :
Oracle PL/SQL Developer Certified Associate (OCA)
Oracle Forms Developer Certified Professional (OCP)
Oracle Database: SQL Certified Expert (OCE) Oracle
 Certified Professional, Java SE 6 Programmer (SCJP)
 Oracle Certified Expert, Java EE 6 Web Component

Developer (SCWCD)
Read more at https://books2read.com/ap/ R3Lm35/Mohammed-Azzam.